# IS GOD
# SPEAKING
# TO ME?

## LYSA TERKEURST

**HARVEST HOUSE PUBLISHERS**
EUGENE, OREGON

Unless otherwise indicated, verses marked NIV are taken from the Holy Bible, New International Version®, NIV®. Copyright © 1973, 1978, 1984, 2011 by Biblica, Inc.® Used by permission. All rights reserved worldwide.

Verses marked MSG are taken from THE MESSAGE, copyright © 1993, 2002, 2018 by Eugene H. Peterson. Used by permission of NavPress. All rights reserved. Represented by Tyndale House Publishers, Inc.

Verses marked NLT are taken from the Holy Bible, New Living Translation, copyright © 1996, 2004, 2015 by Tyndale House Foundation. Used by permission of Tyndale House Publishers, Inc., Carol Stream, Illinois 60188. All rights reserved.

Cover design by Proverbs 31

**Is God Speaking to Me?**
Taken from *What Happens When Women Say Yes to God* © 2007
Published by Harvest House Publishers
Eugene, Oregon 97408
www.harvesthousepublishers.com

ISBN 978-0-7369-8262-7 (pbk.)
ISBN 978-0-7369-8263-4 (eBook)

Library of Congress Cataloging-in-Publication Data is on file at the Library of Congress, Washington, DC.

**All rights reserved.** No part of this publication may be reproduced, stored in a retrieval system, or transmitted in any form or by any means—electronic, mechanical, digital, photocopy, recording, or any other—except for brief quotations in printed reviews, without the prior permission of the publisher.

**Printed in the United States of America**

20  21  22  23  24  25  26  27  / BP-GL /  10  9  8  7  6  5  4  3  2  1

# Contents

# A Letter from Lysa

Hi friend,

Have you ever wondered if God still speaks to us today? Or even more so…whether what you're hearing is really God speaking to you, or just your own thoughts?

I understand. I've wrestled through these very same questions. But what I've discovered through my own study of Scripture is that God absolutely does still speak to us through His Word (2 Timothy 3:16), through His son, Jesus (Hebrews 1:1-2), and through the Holy Spirit that lives in us as believers (John 14:16-17, 1 Corinthians 3:16).

Yes, the Lord is speaking to us and inviting us into a more satisfying relationship with Him than we've ever known before. And our job is to respond in obedience. But you don't have to learn how to do this alone!

What you're holding in your hands is a collection of words that could change the very way you live your life. These crucial chapters are taken from my book *What Happens When Women Say Yes to God*, and it was written after a season of learning how to do just that. If you resonate with what you read here, I hope you'll pick up a copy of the book.

I pray that this will be the starting place and inspiration for you to live a radically obedient life that honors God. What happens when women say yes to God? We are changed in the most beautiful of ways. I've often said people may not care to meet our Jesus until they meet the reality of Jesus working in us and through us. There's no better sermon for the world to encounter than a soul who lives saying yes to God.

Forever changed by saying yes,

*Lysa*

# A Soul That Longs for More

*Whatever God says, do it.*

I t all started several years ago on the day God told me to give away my Bible.

I was exhausted from traveling and speaking. All I wanted to do was to get to my assigned seat on the plane and settle in for a nap. Imagine my absolute delight at being the only person seated in my row. I was just about to close my eyes when two last-minute passengers made their way to my row and took their seats.

Reluctantly, I decided to forgo my nap. The last thing I needed was to fall asleep and snore or, worse yet, wake up with my head resting on the shoulder of the guy beside me. No, I didn't need another most embarrassing moment, so I pulled a manuscript out of my bag and started reading.

"What are you working on?" the guy asked. I told him I was a writer and I was working on a book about leading women to the heart of God. He smiled and said he

thought God was a very interesting topic. I agreed and asked him a few questions about his beliefs. Before long, I found myself reaching into my bag and pulling out my Bible, walking him through some key verses that dealt with the issues he was facing. He kept asking questions, and I kept praying God would give me answers.

All of a sudden, I felt God tugging at my heart to give this man my Bible. Now, this was not just any Bible. This was my everyday, highlighted, underlined, written in, and tearstained Bible. My kids had even drawn pictures in this Bible. I started to argue with God in my head, but His message was clear. I was to give away my Bible.

I emptied it of some old church bulletins and other papers, took a deep breath, sighed, and placed it in the man's hands. "I'd like for you to have my Bible," I said. Astonished, he started to hand it back to me, saying he couldn't possibly accept such a gift. "God told me to give it to you," I insisted. "Sometimes the God of the universe pauses in the midst of all His creation to touch the heart of one person. Today, He paused for you."

The man took my Bible and made two promises. First, he said he would read it, and, second, someday he would pass it on, doing for someone else what I had done for him.

Before I knew it, the plane landed and we were saying our goodbyes. As I stepped into the aisle preparing to disembark, the woman on the other side of the businessman reached out and grabbed my arm. She had been

staring out the window the entire time we were flying, and I thought she'd been ignoring us. But her tearstained face told a different story. In a tone so hushed I could barely hear her, she whispered, "Thank you. What you shared today has changed my life."

I put my hand on hers and whispered back, "You're welcome." Then a knot caught in my throat as tears welled up in my eyes. I didn't have another Bible to give away, so I gave her one of my books and hugged her goodbye. It has been said that we are to tell the whole world about Jesus, using words only if necessary. I saw this powerful truth come to life. Though I never spoke to this lady about Jesus, she saw Him through my obedience. How humbling. How profound.

As I got off the plane that day, I could barely hold back my tears. Three people's hearts were radically changed. I believe the businessman came to know Jesus as his Lord and Savior. I believe the same is true for the lady. But my heart was changed in a dramatic way as well. While on the one hand I was overjoyed at what God had done, I was also brokenhearted by the flood of thoughts that came to mind recounting times I'd told God *no*. How tragic to miss God's divine appointments. I just kept wondering, *How many times have I told You* no, *God? How many times because I was too tired, too insecure, too uncertain, too busy, or too selfish have I walked right past Your divine appointment for me and missed experiencing You?* I lifted up my heart to the Lord and whispered, "Please forgive me for all those times I've said *no*. Right now I say *yes*, Lord. I say yes to You before I even know what You might ask me to do. I simply want You to see a yes-heart in me."

Several minutes after exiting the plane, I was weaving in and out of the crowds, trying to find my connecting gate, when I spotted the businessman again. He stopped me to tell me he had been praying to God and thanking Him for what happened on the plane. We swapped business cards, and, though we lived several states apart, I knew we would stay in touch.

About a month later he called to tell me his life had totally changed. He'd taken a week off from work to read the Bible, and he'd already shared his testimony with numerous people. When he said this to me, my mouth dropped open. I couldn't bring myself to tell him that I'd never taken a week off from work to read the Bible. God was definitely pursuing this man in a serious way! When I asked him what his favorite verse was, he said it was Proverbs 3:5-6: "Trust in the LORD with all your heart; and lean not on your own understanding; in all your ways acknowledge him, and he will make your paths straight." I thought to myself, *Wow! Look at how God has already answered that for my new friend.*

He also told me that after reading the Scriptures he knew he needed to get involved in a church, so he'd decided to visit a large church in his town. On his way there he passed another church, and a strong feeling came over him to turn his car around and go back to that church. So he did. When he got to his seat in the sanctuary, he opened up his bulletin and gasped. Inside the bulletin he saw my picture and an announcement that I was to be the speaker at an upcoming women's conference. He said he felt as though, once again, God had paused just for him.

That day on the plane, when God impressed on my heart to give this man my Bible, I did not know what would happen. This man might have thrown my Bible into the nearest airport trash can, for all I knew. Normally, I would have come up with a hundred reasons *not* to give my Bible away, but that day something changed in me. That day, for the first time, I truly heard the call of a woman who says yes to God: "Whatever God says to do, do it."

## A Fresh Invitation

When I said yes that day, I caught a glimpse of eternity. I saw how beautiful it is when God says to do something and it is done. And I thought, *Why wait for heaven? Why not say yes to God on this side of eternity?*

Oh, friend, the call to become a woman who says yes to God is the fresh invitation your soul is looking for. We all feel a tug at our heart and a stirring in our soul for more, but we are often afraid to venture past our comfort zone. Outside our comfort zone, though, we experience the true fullness of God.

I think at this point it's important for me to paint

an accurate picture of what my life looks like on a daily basis—in case you're imagining me as a woman who is perfectly calm, amazingly organized, incredibly disciplined, and who spends hours upon hours on her knees in solemn solitude before the Lord. Let me assure you, that's not how it is. I am a wife, mom of five adult children, and president of a ministry. I can often be found literally rushing from one thing to the next. My to-do list rarely gets fully accomplished. My emotions have been known to run wild, and my patience can easily run thin. I get pushed to the limit by everyday aggravations. There never seems to be enough time or energy to get everything done or deal with all the chaotic scenarios that come my way.

Can you relate? Great! You are a woman perfectly equipped to say yes to God. Notice I didn't say you're a perfect woman. But if you're in the thick of living with all that life throws at you and you simply whisper yes, you are equipped. "Yes, Lord. I want Your patience to invade my desire to fly off the handle." "Yes, Lord. I want Your perspective to keep my emotions in check." "Yes, Lord. I want Your provision so little things don't overwhelm me." "Yes, Lord. I want Your courage to do what I feel You calling me to do." "Yes, Lord. I want and need more of You in every moment."

You don't need perfect circumstances to be a woman who says yes to God. You don't need the perfect Christlike attitude or all the answers to big theological questions. You simply have to surrender all that's clamoring for attention with the answer God is longing to hear spill from your lips: "Yes, God."

Each day when I wake up, I pray a very simple prayer even before my feet hit the floor. *God, I want to see You. God, I want to hear You. God, I want to know You. God, I want to follow hard after You. And even before I know what I will face today, I say yes to You.* This simple act of surrender each morning will prepare your eyes to see Him, your ears to hear Him, your mind to perceive Him, and your heart to receive Him. This is how to live expecting to experience God.

We have become so familiar with God yet so unaware of Him. We make the mysterious mundane. We construct careful reasons for our rules and sensible whys for our behavior. All the while our soul is longing for a richer experience—one that allows us to escape the limits of sight, sound, touch, taste, and smell and journey to a place of wild, wonder, and passion.

Women who say yes to God are drawn in and embraced by a love like no other. They don't have to wait until the next time they're in church to experience God because they sense God's presence all around them, all through their day. Instead of merely walking through the motions of life, they pursue the adventure of the moment-by-moment divine lessons and appointments God has in store for them. They *expect* to see God, to hear from Him, and to be absolutely filled by His peace and joy—and, therefore, they do and they are.

A woman who says yes to God isn't afraid to be honest with God. Recently, I woke up feeling drained and overwhelmed. I couldn't quite put my finger on the source of my anxiety, but I couldn't shake it, either. As I prayed my normal prayer of wanting to see and hear God, I told Him honestly that I really needed to see evidence of Him in my day.

Later on I was in my kitchen washing dishes, getting dinner ready, and talking with one of my sons. My attention was focused on my son while my hands were just going through the motions of my tasks. Suddenly I felt God's strong impression on my heart to look down in the sink before I reached for another dish. As I did, I saw a very sharp butcher knife sticking blade up inside a glass. Immediately, I knew God's presence was there. I closed my eyes and thanked Him. More than just for sparing my hand from serious injury, I thanked Him for caring enough to be so real in my life.

Sensing a holy God in the middle of life's mundane activities will change your life. But you might not always feel happy about the changes. Being a woman who says yes to God doesn't mean you'll suddenly live happily ever after. Even as I was working on a writing project recently, I had a moment where I simply wanted to throw my hands in the air, toss my computer out the window, and cry out to God, "You have hurt my feelings, and I'm just a little unnerved and upset!"

I was on a retreat at a friend's lake house where I had three days during which I'd hoped to accomplish a lot of writing. I was under a tight deadline for this project and really needed to make a big dent in the task before me. The first day of the retreat went great. I wrote almost 2,000 words, and the friends who were with me loved what I'd written. I went to bed excited about all I'd accomplished so far. Visions of a completed manuscript and my editor's praises danced in my dreams all night long. I woke up the next morning ready to tackle another huge chunk of writing, but first I wanted to admire my accomplishment from the day before. But when I opened up my documents file, the manuscript was nowhere to be found.

Refusing to panic, I asked for my friends' help. They felt confident we could locate the document I'd saved three times the night before. After two hours of searching, one of my friends gently looked at me and verbalized the truth we'd all come to know. "It's gone, Lysa. You're going to have to start over."

*Wait just a minute*. I'd said yes to God that day and had a great quiet time. *I just know He can and will help me find the document,* I thought. But for whatever reason, my document was gone and God had chosen not to bring it back. Tears filled my eyes as bitterness started to creep into my heart. Why would God allow this? My friend could sense my despair and gently replied, "Lysa, look at this loss as a sacrifice of praise to God. It is so hard in today's abundance to give God a true sacrifice, but losing 2,000 words and a whole day's work would qualify. Give this to Him without feeling bitter."

I resisted glaring at my well-meaning friend as she then broke into singing an old favorite, "We bring a sacrifice of praise into the house of the Lord…" By the second stanza I actually found myself humming. I wasn't quite ready to sing, but humming got me going in a better direction. Being a woman who says yes to God means making the choice to trust Him even when you can't understand His requirements. It also means that once you've said yes to God, you refuse to turn back, even when things get hard.

This kind of obedience invites you to embrace a bigger vision for your life. When you look at your everyday circumstances through the lens of God's perspective, you come to see each situation, each person who crosses your path, each encounter with Him as a divine appointment. Each day counts, and every action and reaction matters. God absolutely loves to take ordinary people and do extraordinary things in them, through them, and with them.

## A Party in Your Honor

Imagine you're planning a wonderful surprise party for someone you dearly love. You've made the plans, invited all the guests, and decided on the menu. You can't wait for the big moment when all the guests yell,

"Surprise!" and your loved one finally joins in the festivities. You know she'll understand just how cherished and adored she is when she sees everything that's been done in her honor.

Finally, the time for the surprise arrives. All of the guests are waiting in anticipation at the front door. You see your loved one pull into the driveway, and you hear the car engine turn off. As she opens the car door, you see the interior lights come on while she gathers her things. Your heart races as you see her heading up the driveway. Suddenly, she makes an unusual turn and heads to the back door.

You quickly make your way to the back door to redirect her. Your cheerful greeting is met with a halfhearted smile, and your attempts to send her to the front door are brushed aside. She insists she is tired and will look at what you want to show her tomorrow. Only you know that tomorrow the guests will be gone, the leftover food will be stored away, and the party will be over.

How sad for the guest of honor who missed her own surprise party! And how disappointing for the party planner who orchestrated the event.

God must feel the same way when we miss the "surprise parties"—the divine appointments—that await us each day. How it must disappoint Him when we don't hear or don't listen to Him redirecting us to the front door. How it must grieve Him when we walk through our lives oblivious of His activity all around us. How it must break

His heart when we brush aside something that not only would make us feel special and noticed by God, but also would allow us to join Him in making life a little sweeter for others.

How many times have we missed our own surprise party?

God reveals Himself and His activity to all of us, but very few really want an encounter with Him. Divine encounters cause extreme changes in our plans, our perspectives, and our personhood, and most of us hate change. But protecting ourselves from change only leads to boredom.

As I've traveled around the country speaking at conferences, I am amazed and saddened by the number of people missing out on the most exciting part of being a Christian—experiencing God. Over and over people tell me they want something more in their Christian life. They want to recognize God's voice, live in expectation of His activity, and embrace a life totally sold out for Him. I suspect that tucked in the corner of your heart is the same desire. And I've discovered that the key to having this kind of incredible adventure is radical obedience.

## The Road That Leads to Blessing

You may be surprised to discover that radical obedience is not really that radical. It is really biblical obedience—but we've strayed so far from biblical obedience that saying yes now seems radical. In today's society, it is radical to obey God's commands, listen to the Holy Spirit's convictions, and walk in Jesus' character. But we will never experience the radical blessings God has in store for us without radical obedience. It is the road that leads to blessing. It is what happens when women say yes to God.

And you won't find the full blessing until you give walking in obedience your full attention. Obedience, however, is more than just "not sinning." It is having the overwhelming desire to walk in the center of God's will at every moment. Don't stumble over fearing you won't be perfect or that you are sure to mess up. Saying yes to God isn't about perfect performance, but rather perfect surrender to the Lord day by day. Your obedience becomes radical the minute this desire turns into real action. Radical obedience is hearing from God, feeling His nudges, participating in His activity, and experiencing His blessings in ways few people ever do.

If this is what you want, read on.

## Seven Simple Words

After hearing about the day I gave away my Bible, people often ask me if I've ever gotten it back. It always makes me laugh a little because, to be honest, I don't want to get that Bible back (or any of the Bibles I've given away since then)—at least not for a very long time. I've had this vision of one day being on a plane when I'm old and gray, and the person next to me starts talking. She tells me of the amazing things God has done in her life since the day she received a Bible from a stranger who had received it from another stranger who had received it from another stranger. She'll then reach inside her bag and pull out a worn and tattered book I've held once before. Wow, what a day that will be!

The man I gave the Bible to that day has continued to share his testimony, and I still hear from others whose lives have been changed because of his story. Recently, a lady wrote to tell me that the "Bible man" opened up a business meeting she attended by sharing how God had changed his life:

> I just finished visiting with a friend of yours and mine. His name is Ron. Over the years I have seen him struggling with his success and the decisions in his life. Today, Ron is filled with a different spirit. Your actions brought him back in touch with God. He shared his story with the office on how he met you and the effect of your actions. Isn't it strange that we know God is powerful and we know that we should listen, but sometimes we shut Him out? I can't explain the emotion I felt when I heard this story, but I can tell you that I am seeking some way to be more active in spreading God's Word. Bless you and bless Ron for being wonderful messengers.

Don't we all long to see God at work? His activity around us, in us, and through us is the greatest adventure there is. The God of the universe wants to use you!

There is but one requirement for this adventure. We have to set *our* rules and agendas aside—our dos and don'ts, our social graces and proper places—and follow God's command. His one requirement is so simple and yet so profound: *Whatever God says to do, do it.* That's it. That is the entire Bible, Old Testament and New, hundreds of pages, thousands of verses, all wrapped up in seven words.

It is the call of the radically obedient woman who makes the choice to say yes to God.

## Living Out Your "Yes"

Did the story about the man on the airplane and giving him the Bible inspire you? How?

What is holding you back from going deeper in your relationship with God?

- Time?
- Intimidation?

- Not feeling like the Bible applies to your everyday life?
- Seems too hard?

Comment on one or more of the above or another thing you sense holding you back.

Psalm 19:7-10 says:

> The law of the LORD is perfect, refreshing the soul. The statutes of the LORD are trustworthy, making wise the simple. The precepts of the LORD are right, giving joy to the heart. The commands of the LORD are radiant, giving light to the eyes. The fear of the LORD is pure, enduring forever. The decrees of the LORD are firm, and all of them are righteous. They are more precious than gold, than much pure gold; they are sweeter than honey, than honey from the honeycomb.

I also love how Eugene Peterson paraphrases this same passage in *The Message*:

The revelation of GOD is whole and pulls our lives together. The signposts of GOD are clear and point out the right road. The life-maps of GOD are right, showing the way to joy. The directions of GOD are plain and easy on the eyes. GOD's reputation is twenty-four-carat gold, with a lifetime guarantee. The decisions of GOD are accurate down to the nth degree. God's Word is better than a diamond, better than a diamond set between emeralds. You'll like it better than strawberries in spring, better than red, ripe strawberries.

List what Psalm 19:7-10 promises about God's Word.

The resolve of the human spirit is truly an amazing thing. We will fight to the death for something we want to protect, truly believe in, or desire. So why would we be lackadaisical about the most eternally significant relationship there is?

Read Deuteronomy 6:5.

- How can you love God with your heart?

- How can you love God with your soul?
- How can you love God with your strength?

Is there something you might need to let go of in order to have the freedom to say yes to God?

- Fear that it may cost you too much?
- Uncertain that you will like what a life sold out to Christ looks like?
- Feeling insecure that you'll be able to go the distance?

Psalm 16:7-9 (NLT) says,

> I will bless the LORD who guides me; even at night my heart instructs me. I know the LORD is always with me. I will not be shaken, for he is right beside me. No wonder my heart is filled with joy, and my mouth shouts his praises! My body rests in safety.

Write below how this verse gives a sure answer for each concern listed above:

In this chapter we read, "Being a woman who says yes to God means making the choice to trust Him even when you can't understand why He requires some of the things He does. It also means that once you've said yes to God, you refuse to turn back even when things get hard."

Write out a personal prayer of commitment for your new adventure with God:

# Two

# Hearing God's Voice

*God wants us to live in expectation
of hearing from Him.*

received this letter from Neil in the British Isles.

Dear Lysa,

It's winter in the U.K. My wife bought me an exercise bike for my forty-ninth birthday so I could commit to getting my weight down.

While I pedal, I turn on U.C.B. Europe radio [the Christian radio broadcast]. One morning I caught the final part of your story about the Bible man and the plane journey. I just wept right on through. The program repeats in the evening, so I taped it and listened to it again with my wife, and we both wept.

In the 26 years I've claimed to be a Christian, I think my witness has deteriorated. Your message has inspired me to try again. I realize that the time is short and the Lord is coming.

The man who delivers my coal knocked at the door today. He has been sick for several weeks, and he is only 42. I asked him what the problem had been. He has a brain hemorrhage. He went on to tell me that it had made him think about life. I asked him if he had a faith, but he didn't answer. So I shared briefly. It was off the cuff, but next week I'll be "preprayered" for him.

I've decided I will try to hear God's prompt-ings and remember my time is not my own.

Every day, God speaks to us. Sometimes He invites us to draw close and listen as He reveals Himself, His char-acter, and His direction. Other times He calls to us to par-ticipate in His purposes—for example, Neil sharing with the man who delivers his coal. Still other times He simply whispers to remind us of His amazing love for us.

Oh, what joy it is to know God speaks to me! But I've found that many believers are missing this vital ele-ment in their relationship with Him. As I've talked with people about my own radical obedience journey, they are quick to ask how they might hear from God too. Maybe you have some of these same questions: How do I know if God is speaking to me? How do I discern whether it is His voice speaking or just my own idea? What if I feel God is telling me to do something that doesn't seem to make sense?

There is no magic formula for being able to discern God's voice. We can *learn* to recognize it the way we recognize the voices of those close to us: by knowing Him. And when we know Him, we can tell if what we're feeling led to do is from Him or not.

Though I hear from God all the time, I've never heard His voice audibly. When God speaks to me, it is a certain impression on my heart that I've come to recognize as Him. I've also learned to ask five key questions to help me determine if what I'm hearing is from God or not:

1. Does what I'm hearing line up with Scripture?
2. Is it consistent with God's character?
3. Is it being confirmed through messages I'm hearing at church or studying in my quiet time?
4. Is it beyond me?
5. Would it please God?

Asking these questions helps me tell the difference between my thoughts and God's impressions. Let's look at each of these to unpack what they mean a little bit further.

## Does What I'm Hearing Line Up with Scripture?

God will not speak to us or tell us to do something that is contrary to His Word. But unless we know Scripture, we will not be able to discern whether what we are hearing is consistent or not with the Word. The apostle Paul wrote, "Do not conform any longer to the pattern of this world, but be transformed by the renewing of your mind. Then you will be able to test and approve what God's will is—his good, pleasing and perfect will" (Romans 12:2). God's Word is the language the Holy Spirit uses to help us understand what God is speaking to our hearts. We must get into God's Word and let God's Word get into us. This will transform our mind and prepare it for whatever God wants to tell us. Then, as Paul wrote, we will be able to test and approve not just God's good will, and not just His pleasing will, but His perfect will.

The good news is that you don't need a seminary degree to read your Bible. If reading God's Word is new for you, choose a translation that is easy to understand with a built-in commentary. A good rule of thumb is "Simply Start and Start Simply." Read a passage of Scripture and ask yourself: Who is this passage speaking to? What is it saying to me? What direction is this passage giving? How might I need to change my way of thinking or acting as a result of this verse? What are some other verses that relate to this topic, both in the Old Testament and New Testament?

These questions are just a starting place. I encourage you to get a journal and start recording the verses you study and some of your personal experiences with the things you are learning as you read God's Word.

## Is What I'm Hearing Consistent with God's Character?

God's Word also provides rich information regarding His character. As you come across verses revealing aspects of God's nature, make note of them. Just as God always speaks in accordance with His Word, He speaks in accordance with His character. God will not say things that are inconsistent with who He is. The apostle Paul writes, "Those who live according to the sinful nature have their minds set on what that nature desires; but those who live in accordance with the Spirit have their minds set on what the Spirit desires" (Romans 8:5). What is it that God's Spirit desires? Answering this question helps us understand God's character.

We find great insight into God's character in Galatians 5:22-23: "The fruit of the Spirit is love, joy, peace, patience, kindness, goodness, faithfulness, gentleness and self-control." These characteristics in a person's life are the evidence of Christ at work. As one study Bible puts it, "The fruit of the Spirit is the spontaneous work of the Holy Spirit in us. The Spirit produces these character traits that are found in the nature of Christ. They are by-products of Christ's control—we can't obtain them by trying to get them without his help. If we want the fruit of the Spirit to grow in us, we must join our lives to his. We must know him, love him, remember him, and imitate him."[1] If the fruit of the Spirit is our imitation of Him, then it must be consistent with God's character.

When you feel God speaking to you, ask yourself: Is what I am hearing consistent with God's love, joy, peace, etc.?

In addition to the fruit of the Spirit, God's character is revealed in a loving relationship with us. As we experience God personally, we come to know new names for Him. When we've experienced His provision, we come to know Him as our Provider. When we've experienced His comfort, we come to know Him as our Comforter. When we've experienced His amazing love, we come to know Him as the Great Lover of our souls. The longer we know Him and the more we experience Him personally, the more we learn about His character.

If what you're hearing is consistent with God's character, ask the next question.

## Is What I'm Hearing Being Confirmed Through Other Messages?

When God is speaking to me about a particular issue, I cannot escape it. Around every corner there is a sermon, podcast episode, speaker's topic, or conversation with a friend that is consistent with what I've been hearing from God in my time alone with Him.

Do you spend time alone with God? We shouldn't wait to hear from God just on Sunday mornings or during a weekly Bible study or when we attend a conference.

These are places to confirm what we've heard in our time alone, where we are personally studying God's Word, learning more about His character, and listening for His voice.

Think about having a conversation with another person. You both speak and you both listen. The same is true with our conversations with the Lord when we're one-on-one with Him. We shouldn't be doing all the talking. God wants us to pour out our hearts to Him, and then He wants to respond to us. Jesus shared this parable:

> The watchman opens the gate for him, and the sheep listen to his voice. He calls his own sheep by name and leads them out. When he has brought out all his own, he goes on ahead of them, and his sheep follow him because they know his voice (John 10:3-4).

Now let's reread this verse with some clarifying remarks added in.

> The watchman [Jesus] opens the gate [a way for us to have direct communication with God] for him, and the sheep [you and I] listen to his voice. He [Jesus] calls his own sheep by name [He speaks to us personally] and leads them out [providing us with direction]. When he has brought out all his own, he goes on ahead of them, and his sheep follow him because they

know his voice [they know His voice because
they have spent time with Him] (John 10:3-4).

Jesus is the one who provides a way for us to be able to
talk with God and hear from God. God calls us by name.
He wants to have a personal connection with each of us.
Think about when you call someone's name. You know
that person. You are calling on them so the two of you
can connect in some way. This verse is telling us that the
way God wants to connect with us is to provide direction
for us in life. He has gone before us and sees the dangers
and trials we will face. He is telling us the way to go, the
perspectives to keep, the things to avoid, and the things
to hold fast to. Most of all He is speaking to us because
we are His own and He wants a relationship with us. He
loves us, adores us, treasures us, and has a good plan for
us. He longs for us to know His voice and listen to His
voice. The only way to know and trust God in this way is
to spend time with Him.

As a parent, I've expected the same thing from my
children. I know things they don't, and I can perceive dangers they are oblivious to. I want them to listen to me, but
not because I want to exert a sense of authority in their life
and simply boss them around. No, I want them to listen
because I love them, adore them, treasure them, and want
only the best for them. When they were younger, even
when they didn't understand the why behind my instruc-
tions or like the limitations I put in place, I wanted them

to be obedient because they trusted me and they loved me. The same is true in our relationship with our heavenly Parent.

When we invest in spending time alone with God, He will speak to us, and what we hear from Him in these quiet times will be echoed in other places. Listen for God's voice and then look for the message to be confirmed. If it is, you're ready to ask the fourth question.

## Is What I'm Hearing Beyond Me?

When God leads or prompts us to do something small, we will be able to do it if we're willing. But sometimes God calls us to do something big that we feel we can't do in our own strength—either it is beyond our ability or beyond our natural human desire. It is not something we can strategize and manipulate into being in and of ourselves. It can only happen by God's divine intervention. The beauty of doing things beyond ourselves is that we will know it was by God's doing and His alone. And to Him we give all the glory.

I remember when God called me to write my first book. It seemed so exciting and thrilling to think of accomplishing this huge life goal. I envisioned the cover with my name on it. I delighted in imagining the first time I would walk into a bookstore and quietly say to myself, *I wrote that.* The excitement carried me through writing the first 10,000 words. Everything was clicking right along…until I got a note from my editor after she read my first installment. Her two-page, single-spaced feedback can be summed up in two shocking words, "Start over."

I got down on the floor beside my desk, buried my face into the carpet, and cried. "I can't do this, God. I can't write a whole book. What was I thinking? I'm not an author. I'm an imposter who somehow got lucky enough to fool this publisher with my proposal. But now they've seen the real me and think I'm a fool."

Did you notice an often-repeated word in my cries to God? "I'm not." "I can't." "I'm a fool." It was all about me and my inadequacies until I turned the statements into "God is." "God can." "God has called me; therefore, I am equipped."

If God is calling you to do something you feel is beyond you, you are in good company. God has a history of calling people to things that were beyond themselves. Pastor Rick Warren put it this way:

> Abraham was old, Jacob was insecure, Leah was unattractive, Joseph was abused, Moses stuttered, Gideon was poor, Samson was code-pendent, Rahab was immoral, David had an affair and all kinds of family problems, Elijah was suicidal, Jeremiah was depressed, Jonah was reluctant, Naomi was a widow, John the Baptist was eccentric to say the least, Peter was impulsive and hot-tempered, Martha worried

a lot, the Samaritan woman had several failed
marriages, Zachaeus was unpopular, Thomas
had doubts, Paul had poor health, and Timothy was timid. That's quite a group of misfits,
but God used each of them in his service. He
will use you too.[2]

Don't look at your inabilities and dwell in insecurities.
Look at the Almighty God. See this call as the opportunity to watch Him work in you and through you. If you
answer yes to the question *Is this beyond me?* chances are
God is speaking.

## Would What I'm Hearing Please God?

It's easy to talk ourselves out of thinking we've heard
from God. I think we'll pretty much use any excuse to con-
vince ourselves it's not His voice so we don't need to act.
But there's one very important question to ask when we
feel prompted to do something, one question that takes
away our excuses: Would this please God? You see, if what
you are doing pleases God, then even if what you thought
you heard from Him wasn't His voice, you still please Him.
We should always seek to err on the side of pleasing God.
Ask this question, and you'll know what to do.

These five questions are your starting place. The more
you practice listening for God's voice, the more it becomes
a natural part of your daily life. And here's the best news
of all: God *wants* you to hear Him. He wants your faith to
grow. He's told us so over and over in Scripture.

This is my prayer: that your love may abound more and more in knowledge and depth of insight (Philippians 1:9).

This is to my Father's glory, that you bear much fruit, showing yourselves to be my disciples (John 15:8).

We ought always to thank God for you, brothers, and rightly so, because your faith is growing more and more, and the love every one of you has for each other is increasing (2 Thessalonians 1:3).

For this very reason, make every effort to add to your faith goodness; and to goodness, knowledge (2 Peter 1:5).

Finally, brothers, we instructed you how to live in order to please God, as in fact you are living. Now we ask you and urge you in the Lord Jesus to do this more and more (1 Thessalonians 4:1).

## Living Out the Five-Question Filter

My conversations with God are more than a spiritual exercise for me. They are a lifeline. Growing up in my early childhood, I did not have a dad who was very involved in my life. I was desperate to know that I was loved. I remember watching other little girls with their dads and wondering what was so wrong with me that my dad didn't adore me the way theirs did. Maybe it was because I wasn't pretty enough. Maybe I wasn't smart enough. Maybe he had never wanted me.

I was blessed to have another man adopt me as his own when my mom remarried. Charles has been a wonderful father to me who has loved me as his own. However, not having my biological father's love and acceptance left a hole in my heart. Often a little girl's sense of self-worth will be based on her father's love. And her opinion of God will often be based on her opinion of her earthly father.

Both of these were skewed for me. My sense of self-worth was severely lacking. I defined myself as an unwanted, unlovely, throwaway person. I viewed God as a distant, cold ruler who had somehow deemed me unworthy. Many years into my adult life, I came to see a different picture of God. He wooed me and loved me to a place where I finally surrendered my heart to Him. Then a miracle happened…He redefined my identity.

I was no longer a throwaway child. I was a holy and dearly loved daughter of the Most High King. I truly became a brand-new creation. I found the love and acceptance that had been so lacking in my early childhood. That little girl in me craved to spend time with the dad I had missed out on for so long. He whispered to my heart that I was pretty and special and smart, and, best of all, that I was loved.

As a result of knowing what it feels like to be aban-

doned as a child, I have always had a tender place in my
heart for the orphaned child. But after having three biological daughters of my own, I brushed aside any notion
of adopting. That was until one unsuspecting day when
God connected my family with two teenage boys from
the war-torn country of Liberia, Africa. This meeting
changed my family forever as God so clearly whispered
to our hearts that they were to become part of our family.

As soon as I heard His whisper, my mind raced
through the five-question filter.

1. Does what I'm hearing line up with Scripture?
2. Is it consistent with God's character?
3. Is it being confirmed through messages I'm hearing at church or studying in my quiet time?
4. Is it beyond me?
5. Would it please God?

God is very clear in Scripture that as Christians we are
to take care of widows and orphans (James 1:27; Exodus
22:22-23; Isaiah 1:17). Just a few weeks before meeting the
boys I recorded the following verse in my journal: "Reli-
gion that God our Father accepts as pure and faultless is
this: to look after orphans and widows in their distress and
to keep oneself from being polluted by the world" (James
1:27). I had no idea why I was drawn to write this verse
in my journal, but God knew. He made sure I was familiar with an answer to my first filter question. Yes, adopting the boys absolutely lined up with Scripture. And in

the same verse God answered the second question. God defines part of His character as "God our Father." I saw that God had been a Father to me in my time of need, so I should be willing to be that for someone else in need.

The confirmations were also undeniable. God had been bringing friends into my life who had adopted orphaned children. I never thought it would be something my husband would be open to, and yet God drew his heart to a place of acceptance. My girls begged us to consider adopting and prayed often for big brothers. It seemed everywhere I turned the theme of adopting was staring me in the face. Sermons at church, verses in my quiet times, songs on the radio, and whispers by God to my heart all seemed to be saying the same thing. Yes, adopting these boys was being confirmed.

The fourth question did not require much thought at all. Yes, this was totally beyond me. Having boys was beyond me. I had grown up with all sisters and then had three daughters. I felt very ill-equipped to be a mom of boys—especially teenage boys. Having five kids was beyond me. My schedule was already crazy with three kids. How in the world would I be able to add two more? Financially, this seemed beyond what we could do. Not to mention the host of fears that flooded my brain. What if one of the boys hurt one of my girls or hurt me or had emotional baggage that would take a huge toll on the stability of our family? I would only be willing to do this if I knew beyond a shadow of a doubt that it was God's plan and not my own. Only in His strength would this be possible.

The last question became pivotal in our decision to pursue adopting the boys. More than anything else I desire to please God, but the pull of taking an easier path was incredible with this particular invitation. The tug of believing that my worst fears would surely be waiting on the other side of this step of obedience made me want to run and hide. But the love of God kept my heart stilled, and His constant reassurances kept me on course. We said yes to God, not because we were completely comfortable with adopting, but rather because we completely trusted Him.

His voice was strong and gentle, saying, "Do not fear. Remember how I faced the devil in the wilderness, and how I conquered with the sword of the Spirit, which is the word of God. You too have your quick answer for every fear that evil may present—an answer of faith and confidence in Me. Where possible, say it aloud. The spoken word has power. Look on every fear not as a weakness on your part due to illness or worry, but as a very real temptation to be attacked and overthrown. Does the way seem a stony one? Not one stone can impede your progress. Courage. Face the future, but face it only with a brave and happy heart. Do not seek to see it. You are robbing Faith of her sublime sweetness if you do this. Just know that all is well and that Faith, not seeing but believing, is what will bear you to safety over the stormy waters."[3]

So, we let faith carry us as we faced the future as coura-
geously as we could. We quoted Scripture after Scripture
and reminded God that this was His adventure that we
were simply saying yes to while trusting Him completely.
And you know what we discovered? Sheer joy. Not in the
circumstances that we faced necessarily, but in the absolute assurance that we were being obedient to God and
walking in the very center of His will.

I can honestly tell you on the other side of this great
adoption adventure that I can't imagine my life without
my boys. I am so thankful that I followed God's perfect
plan instead of being lured away by fear and worry. Our
boys are grown men now, and I'm more convinced than
ever that even though they were not born from my body,
they were born from my heart. Maybe that was the purpose of that place in my heart that seemed so much like a
hole when I was younger, but now I see it as the channel
through which God brought my boys home.

Use this five-question filter as a starting place in your
conversations with God. Listening for God's voice and
communicating with Him has not always come natu-
rally to me. To this day I have to seek it by asking for the
desire, discipline, discernment, direction, and delight. I
ask for the desire to want God more than anything else. I
ask for the discipline to make my relationship with Him
top priority. I ask for the discernment to know the difference between my own thoughts and God's voice. I ask
for clear direction at each crossroad in my life. I ask for

my relationship with God to be characterized by sheer delight rather than a sense of duty. Have you ever asked God for this type of relationship with Him? When you ask for these things boldly and live in expectation of hearing from God, you will. In Jeremiah 29:13 God promises, "You will seek me and find me when you seek me with all your heart." Then respond by saying yes to Him and confidently walking in absolute dependence and glorious obedience.

Yes, indeed. I love being a woman who says yes to God.

## Living Out Your "Yes"

Read Romans 12:1-2 in the New International Version. Then, write out a definition for the following:

Living sacrifice:


Pleasing to God:


Do not conform:


The pattern of this world:

Transformed:

Renewing of your mind:

Test and approve God's will:

Now reread these verses and summarize what you can learn from them about discerning God's voice:

List some areas of your life that you currently honor God in:

List some areas that you sense you may need to sacrifice or change:

Are there areas of your life where you've conformed to the world's way of thinking?

How can you renew your mind in these areas?

Find two Scripture verses that might be helpful to memorize as you seek to be renewed in this area. Write those here.

What is the promise from these verses for those who actively seek to be transformed and renewed in the way they think?

Write the five questions for discerning God's voice you
learned in this chapter:

  1.

  2.

  3.

  4.

  5.

Remember, this is not the end-all way for hearing God's
voice. It is simply a starting place. Which of these questions do you find most challenging?

In *The Message*, Eugene Peterson paraphrases Romans
9:25-26 by saying, "Hosea put it well: I'll call nobodies
and make them somebodies; I'll call the unloved and make
them beloved. In the place where they yelled out, 'You're
nobody!' they're calling you 'God's living children.'"
Paul continues,

> How can we sum this up? All those people who
> didn't seem interested in what God was doing
> actually embraced what God was doing as he
> straightened out their lives. And Israel, who
> seemed so interested in reading and talking

about what God was doing, missed it. How could they miss it? Because instead of trusting God, they took over. They were absorbed in what they themselves were doing. They were so absorbed in their "God projects" that they didn't notice God right in front of them, like a huge rock in the middle of the road. And so they stumbled into him and went sprawling. Isaiah (again!) gives us the metaphor for pulling this together: Careful! I've put a huge stone on the road to Mount Zion, a stone you can't get around. But the stone is me! If you're looking for me, you'll find me on the way, not in the way (Romans 9:30-33 MSG).

Yes, God wants us to live in expectation of hearing from Him. Sometimes we'll hear Him giving us direction or pointing us to a divine appointment. Other times we'll glean from Him wisdom, correction, or encouragement. But mostly I pray you'll hear His glorious voice proclaiming, "You are somebody! You are my chosen daughter!"

1. *Life Application Study Bible* (NIV) (Wheaton, IL: Tyndale House Publishers, 1988), 2125.

2. Rick Warren, *The Purpose-Driven Life* (Grand Rapids, MI: Zondervan Publishing House, 2002), 233.

3. A.J. Russell, ed., *God Calling* (Grand Rapids, MI: Spire Books, 2005), 113.

# Three

# Radically Blessed

*You can experience the blessings
of radical obedience.*

The other day I was driving down a busy road when I came upon a traffic light that was both green and red at the same time. I slowed, unsure of what I should do, as did other cars coming from all directions. It was a confusing and dangerous situation. Some people stopped, others ran through the light, and still others pulled off to the side of the intersection.

I finally made it through the intersection and thought about what had just happened. It was as if God were showing me a visual picture of what it's like when a person is indecisive in her obedience to Him. We can't seek to follow God wholeheartedly if part of our heart is being pulled in a different direction. We can't pursue the radically obedient life and still continue to flirt with disobedience in certain areas of our life. We can't be both red and green toward God at the same time. It gets us nowhere. It's confusing. It's dangerous.

This booklet has been your invitation to become a woman who says yes to God and catches a glimpse of the blessings that are ahead. Now it's time to respond.

Now, I know your mind might be flooded with the same questions that flooded my mind as I was responding to this invitation.

"What if I don't feel able to make such a commitment?"

"What if I say yes and then mess up?"

"What if I have times when I just don't feel like being obedient?"

Let's take a moment to consider the source. Who is asking these questions? That's not your voice sowing seeds of doubt; it's Satan's voice. He wants to keep you in doubt and confusion. He wants you to pull off to the side of the intersection and remain ineffective. He wants you to fail to fulfill the purposes God has for you and thwart the positive impact you could make in the lives of so many.

You don't feel able? Good! Christ's power is made perfect through weakness (2 Corinthians 12:9). Ask God for the strength to persevere every day. Ask God for the desire to remain radically obedient and for spiritual eyes to see the radical blessings He will shower upon you.

What if you mess up? Grace! "God opposes the proud but gives grace to the humble. Submit yourselves, then, to God. Resist the devil, and he will flee from you. Come near to God and he will come near to you…humble yourselves before the Lord, and he will lift you up" (James

4:6-8,10). Please don't think I walk this radical obedience journey with perfection, because I don't. Chances are you won't either. But God doesn't expect perfection from us— He expects a person humble enough to admit her weaknesses and committed enough to press through and press on. He will guide us past the doubts and fears and lift us up to fulfill our calling.

What if you wake up in a bad mood and just don't feel like being obedient? Choice! Obey based on your decision to obey, not on your ever-changing feelings. *I don't feel like giving. I don't feel like smiling. I don't feel like listening to God.* But here's what God has to say about that: "It is *God* who works in you to will and to act according to his good purpose" (Philippians 2:13, emphasis added). When we ask God to continually give us the desire to remain obedient, He does. He will help us to want to obey Him and will give us His power to do so.

## Get Ready!

If your answer is no right now to radical obedience, I just ask you to do one thing while you sit at the red light. Pray that God will give you the desire to say yes. Let me challenge you for the next 30 days to pray and ask God to reveal Himself to you and fill you with a desire for Him like never before. Remember that lasting obedience must be born out of desire, not duty. Choose to be a woman who says yes to God by starting with this simple prayer. It will cost you only a minute of your time each day, but it will bless you for a lifetime!

If your answer to this invitation is yes, then get ready. You have not only signed up for the most incredible journey you can imagine, but you've also just given God the green light to pour out His radical blessings on your life! What I'm writing about here is just a glimpse of how God will bless you. He's capable of so much more!

### Deeper Relationship with God

You will begin to live in expectation of hearing from God every day. You will start to better understand His character and seek to be more like Him. You will discover the depth of love that the Father has for you that you never even knew was possible. This will give you a feeling of acceptance and significance that you can't get any other way.

Some people spend their whole lives chasing things they think will make them feel accepted and significant. But the truth is this world only has packages full of empty promises to offer. The new house, the fancier car, the latest gadget, the fastest computer, the sleek fashions, and everything else that seems so enticing won't last. They will all wear out, break down, tear up, and become obsolete. Five, ten, twenty years from now, they won't look so appealing and will have to either be updated or replaced. Fifty years from now, most will be taking up space in a junkyard somewhere.

In contrast, every investment we make in our relationship with God will only serve to reap rich dividends for now and eternity. No time spent experiencing God will ever be a waste.

## More Adventurous Life

I've heard it said that life would not be so hard if it weren't so daily. Yet the Bible says that each day is a gift from God that we should rejoice in (Psalm 118:24). Daily adventures with God will add an excitement to your life that will change your whole perspective. No longer is your day just one task after another, but rather a string of divine appointments and hidden treasures waiting to be discovered.

Seeing life like this opens up God's storehouses of joy. The mark of a truly godly woman is one who reveals the power of God not so much in her doing as in her being. She has opened God's treasure chest of joy and so filled her heart with gratitude and love that just being around her inspires you. She goes about the simplest of tasks, her everyday duties, and even the rough patches of life with such grace that you find yourself wanting to imitate her. She is full of adventure yet not worn out from the journey.

## Depth of Inner Peace

In our world of turmoil and uncertainty, there is nothing more precious than peace. When we say yes to God, we know that our life and the lives of those we love rest in the certainty of His never-changing love for us. While we can't control the circumstances we face, we can choose how we react to them. If you've settled in your heart to say yes to God and completely trust Him, then you don't have to worry about the future. You are not in charge of the outcome, you are simply responsible to be obedient. You will be blessed with the peace of knowing that God has a perfect plan and holds everything in His perfect control. What freedom this brings!

## Personal Satisfaction

Radically obedient people no longer have to strategize and manipulate things into being. Instead, they are blessed with opportunities that bring them real satisfaction according to God's perfect design for them. When my husband and I adopted our sons from Liberia, I thought the responsibility of adding more children would mean the end of my ministry. But that has not been the case. God has grown the ministry, sent more people to help run it, and blessed us with the most amazing opportunities to tell our adoption story. We've been allowed to freely talk about listening and obeying God on *Good Morning America*, *The Today Show*, and other national secular programs. God has taken our obedience and maximized our ministry's impact.

## Better Relationships with People

In every relationship with others, you will find things that you love and things that, to be quite honest, get on your nerves. The radically obedient person is blessed with being able to appreciate another's Christlikeness and to give grace to their humanness. Whether a person is a believer or not, they are still made in God's image

(Genesis 1:26-27), and God is crazy in love with them. When you are committed to radical obedience, you see everyone through God's eyes of love.

### Meaning and Purpose to Life

Author Bruce Wilkinson wrote:

> Once the Lord has fed His child through intimate devotions, He begins to call him more pointedly to deeper obedience. At this point, the believer desires more of the Lord so much that he is more than willing to do whatever the Lord requires…Obedience for this individual is no longer a burden, undertaken only because the Bible tells him to do something. Rather, obedience becomes a joy because his closest friend and most compassionate Lord beckons him to be like Him.[1]

Our hearts search for deeper meaning in life, and radically obedient people find it in loving the Lord, loving others He brings in our path, and continually seeking to become more like Jesus.

### Eternal Perspective

Life is about so much more than just the here and now, and the radically obedient person lives in light of that perspective. Life isn't about being comfortable and taking the easiest route. It's about living to give our lives away and making a real impact in this world. It's not about serving out of religious duty. It's about delighting in our relationship with God so much that we want to serve out of an overflow of love and gratitude. Our time here is but a small dot on an eternal line. What we do now in this brief moment will determine our destiny for eternity. The radically obedient person is blessed with an eternal perspective.

## A Radically Obedient Example

I am drawn to the story of one New Testament woman who was radically obedient—Mary, Lazarus' sister. I am moved by Mary's overwhelming love for Jesus. She was a woman who understood the essence of radical obedience. She knew when to listen and when to act. She knew when to simply sit at the Master's feet and when to pour out all she had in lavish love for her Lord (Matthew 26:6-13).

Jesus had just announced He would be crucified. Mary took what was probably her most costly possession, the perfume from her alabaster jar, and poured it out on Him. Normally, one would pour perfume on a dead body, but Mary anointed Jesus while He was still living. I believe it was so Jesus could carry the scent of her love with Him to the cross.

Mary was scolded by some of the disciples for her act of extravagance, but Jesus was quick to jump to her defense. What others saw as waste, Jesus saw as the purest form of walking out the gospel message. She was willing to love Him without reservation, without concern for what others might think or even concern for herself. Mary showed an unabashed love through this act, and, make no mistake, Jesus was quick to lavish His love right back on her. "I tell you the truth," Jesus said, "wherever the gospel is preached throughout the world, what she has done will also be told, in memory of her" (Matthew 26:13).

Isn't it amazing that such a small act of obedience could have such far-reaching effects? That can happen in our lives as well. Indeed, Mary was radically obedient and radically blessed…and you can be too.

## How It Ends

Well, this whole adventure began with God telling me to give away my Bible, so is it any surprise that it ends the same way? Not too long ago, I was flying to the Washington, DC, area for a speaking engagement. The man next to me on the plane was busy working on his computer and did not appear to be in the mood to be interrupted. My heart kept feeling drawn to share the gospel with him, but it didn't seem appropriate to force a conversation. So I prayed.

I prayed that God would prompt *him* to start talking to me. And talk he did. It wasn't long before he put his computer away and started asking me all kinds of questions about my career. Because I write and speak about Jesus, this was a perfect opportunity to tell him all about my Boss! When we started talking about God, he said he'd been studying the Qur'an and several other religious writings, but not the Bible. However, he'd called the friend he was traveling to see and asked if they could buy a Bible that weekend to complete his collection.

I almost fell out of my seat. Of all the planes traveling to Washington that day and of all the people who were seated together, God arranged for a man who needed a Bible to sit beside a woman who loves to give Bibles away! I shared with my new friend my passion for giving away Bibles, and I promised I would send him one the next week. He sat stunned. When he finally spoke again, he told me he knew this was more than sheer coincidence. He knew God was reaching out to him.

Oh, my friend, we don't have to seek to create opportunities to say yes to God. God has already gone before us and established them. We simply have to respond.

I pray that the end of this booklet is not the conclusion of your journey. I sincerely hope this is only the starting place, the point of inspiration and expression for you to live a radically obedient, radically blessed life. What happens when women say yes to God? The world is changed.

1.  Bruce Wilkinson, *Set Apart* (Sisters, OR: Multnomah Publishers, 1998), 175.

# Living Out Your "Yes"

God's Word has so much to say on the topic of saying yes to Him and the amazing blessings that follow. Pick ten of these key verses, look them up for yourself, and discover what God wants you to know about His calling on your life. I've summarized the verses, but it will be so much more powerful to dig into God's Word and record the powerful promises yourself.

### Deuteronomy 28:1-14
Obedience opens God's storehouse of blessings.

### 2 Chronicles 16:9
God will strengthen the heart of the obedient person.

### Esther 4:14
God has called you to obedience for such a time as this.

### Psalm 15
Obedient people dwell in the presence
and peace of God.

### Psalm 24
Obedience in what you say, what you do, and what you
think leads to holiness and blessings from God.

### Isaiah 55:1-3
Obedience brings your soul satisfaction,
delight, and new life.

### Hosea 10:12
Obedience reaps the fruit of unfailing love and brings showers of righteousness.

### Malachi 3:8-10
Being obedient givers will open God's storehouse of blessing.

### Malachi 3:16-17
Radically obedient people are treasures to God.

### Matthew 26:12-13
Even small acts of obedience have widespread effects.

### Romans 1:5
Obedience comes from faith.

### Romans 6:15-16
Obedience leads to righteousness.

### Romans 8:5-6
Those walking in obedience have their minds set on God's desires.

### 2 Corinthians 9:6
The extent that we sow in obedience will determine the extent we will reap in blessings.

### 2 Corinthians 9:13
Men will praise God for the obedience that accompanies our faith.

### Ephesians 4:24
We were created to be like God. We walk this out in obedience leading to holiness.

### Philippians 2:13
It is God working in us that prompts us to be obedient and fulfill His good purpose.

### Philippians 4:9
What you have learned, heard, or seen from God, walk it out in obedience and you will be blessed with peace.

### 2 Timothy 2:20-21
God is able to use the obedient person for His noblest purposes.

### Hebrews 11
A list of radically obedient, radically blessed people.

### 1 Peter 1:13-14
Prepare your mind for obedience, which leads to holiness.

### 1 Peter 2:21-22
Those who walk in obedience walk in Jesus' footsteps.

### 1 John 2:3-6
Obedience makes God's love complete in us and enables us to walk as Jesus did.

# Go beyond this booklet...

*Your job is obedience. God's job is everything else.*

If you've ever found yourself wondering... *What is God's plan for my life?* or *Can He really use me?* you're not alone. Lysa TerKeurst has wrestled through those same questions. But she's also learned that we were absolutely created to participate in God's divine activity and experience His rich blessings. We just have to say *yes* to Him!

Through her own struggles, doubts, and honest vulnerability, Lysa will equip you to:

- Know what God is speaking personally to you with practical ways to listen for His voice.

- Overcome the fear that you're not doing the Christian life right by learning it's about perfect surrender, not perfect performance.
- Apply key teachings to your own situation today with helpful study questions and reflection prompts.

Get ready for a journey of joy and purpose—one that will radically bless you beyond what you can ask or imagine!

*Available wherever books are sold!*